Rocks and Minerals

Keith Lye

RSVP
RAINTREE
STECK-VAUGHN
P U B L I S H E R S
The Steck-Vaughn Company

Austin, Texas

Editor: A. Patricia Sechi
Design: Shaun Barlow
Project Manager: Joyce Spicer
Electronic Production:
    Scott Melcer
Artwork: Michael Lye
Cover artwork: Michael Lye
Picture Research:
    Ambreen Husain
Educational Advisor:
    Joy Richardson
Consultant: Miranda MacQuitty

Library of Congress
Cataloging-in-Publication Data
Lye, Keith.
    Rocks and minerals / Keith Lye.
        p.   cm. — (What About)
    Includes index.
    Summary: Discusses the different kinds of rocks and minerals, how they are formed, and their various uses.
    Hardcover   ISBN 0-8114-3411-7
    Softcover   ISBN 0-8114-6441-5
    1. Petrology — Juvenile literature.   2. Mineralogy — Juvenile literature.   [1. Rocks
2. Minerals.   3. Petrology.
4. Mineralogy.]   I. Title.   II. Series.
QE432.2.L94 1993
552—dc20   92-31817
                                CIP
                                AC

Printed and bound in the United States by Lake Book, Melrose Park, IL

5 6 7 8 9 0 LB 98 97 96 95

Contents

What Are Rocks?	3
How Are Igneous Rocks Formed?	4
What Is Granite?	6
Sedimentary Rocks	8
Fossils in Rocks	10
"Cooked" Rocks	12
What Are Rocks Made Of?	14
Hard and Soft Minerals	16
Crystals	18
Minerals and Metals	20
Using Rocks and Minerals	22
Valuable Metals	24
Precious Stones	26
Other Stones	28
Things to Do	30
Glossary	31
Index	32

What Are Rocks?

Rocks are the hard parts of the **Earth**. They form the Earth's covering, called the **crust**. Soil and plants cover most rocks. Soil is made of worn bits of rock, such as sand and **clay**, and the remains of dead plants and animals. Rocks have many uses. Some are used in buildings. Others contain valuable metals and **minerals**.

▽ Soil and plants cover most rocks. But we can see rocks in cliffs or where the earth is blasted open for a new road.

3

How Are Igneous Rocks Formed?

Under the Earth's crust it is so hot that some rocks melt. The melted rock is called **magma**. Some of it comes to the surface through openings called **volcanoes**. When magma reaches the surface, it is called lava. The lava cools and hardens to form rock. These rocks are called **igneous rocks**. Basalt is a common igneous rock.

▷ The rocks at Giant's Causeway in Northern Ireland are made of basalt.

▽ Volcanic bombs are lumps of lava. They are hurled out of volcanoes.

▽ Pumice is a volcanic rock which has lots of holes.

△ Obsidian is a glassy rock. It is made from lava that has cooled quickly.

What Is Granite?

Granite is an igneous rock made from magma. The magma cools and hardens below the surface of the Earth. Granite is the most common rock made like this. It only appears on the surface after the rocks above it have been worn away. This happens in many mountain areas. Granite may be white, gray, pink, or red.

◁ Sheets of polished granite can be used to cover the surface of buildings and walls.

◁ Granite is a hard rock. It is often used for curbstones.

◁ Granite is used for sculpture. The granite is polished when the sculpture is finished.

▽ Granite often forms large parts of mountain areas.

Sedimentary Rocks

Many rocks are made from bits of other rocks which have been worn away. These bits are called sediments. Rivers wash them into the sea. On the seafloor the loose sediments are squeezed together. After a very long time they become solid rock. Rocks formed in this way are called **sedimentary rocks**.

▷ Sedimentary rocks usually form in flat layers like a pile of sandwiches.

▽ Conglomerates are rocks made of pebbles set in fine sand or mud.

▷ Sandstone is made from grains of sand.

◁ Shale is formed from fine clay and mud that pile up on the seafloor.

Fossils in Rocks

Animal and plant remains are sometimes buried in sand or mud. When the sand and mud turn into hard rock, these remains may be saved as fossils. Some rocks called limestone are made up of fossils such as seashells. Chalk is a kind of limestone. It is made from the remains of tiny sea creatures.

▽ Miners dig coal from the ground.

▷ Marks made by leaves can be found as fossils in rocks.

▽ Ammonites are ancient sea creatures. Their shells are often found as fossils.

▽ In some limestone rocks the remains of shells are easy to see.

▽ Coal is made of the remains of ancient plants which have been pressed into hard rock.

△ This limestone contains many small fossils.

"Cooked" Rocks

Heat and pressure change rocks. Shale is a rock made from clay. When it is heated and squeezed inside the Earth, it turns into a hard rock called slate. Rocks that have been changed in this way are called **metamorphic rocks**.

▷ Marble is cut out of the Earth at quarries like this one.

▽ This piece of migmatite shows the patterns of the rock as it melted.

▽ Slate is a hard rock formed from soft rock shale.

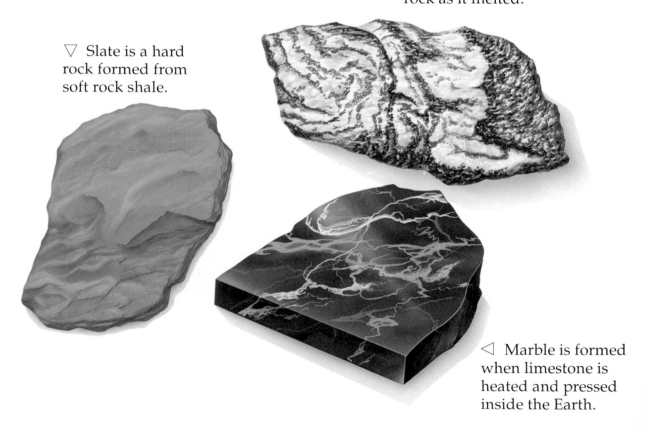

◁ Marble is formed when limestone is heated and pressed inside the Earth.

What Are Rocks Made Of?

Rocks are made of minerals. Some rocks are made of only one mineral. Most rocks are made of more than one kind of mineral. Limestone rocks are made mostly of the mineral calcite. Granite often contains three minerals. These are a pink or gray feldspar, a glassy quartz, and a black mineral called mica.

▽ Chalk is a white limestone. Cliffs of chalk are mainly made up of the mineral calcite.

△ The shiny glassy substance in granite is the mineral quartz.

▽ Feldspar is one of the main minerals found in granite. It may be pink or gray.

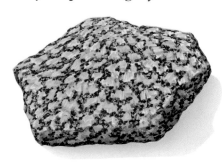

▽ Mica is another one of the main minerals in granite. It has black crystals.

Hard and Soft Minerals

Diamonds are minerals. A diamond is the hardest of all natural things, and it is used for cutting glass. Other minerals such as quartz are also very hard. Some minerals are very soft. Talc is a mineral used to make talcum powder. It is so soft that you can crush it with your fingernail. The hardness of minerals helps us to tell one from another.

▷ Diamonds can be used to cut patterns in glass.

▽ You can scratch the mineral calcite with a copper coin.

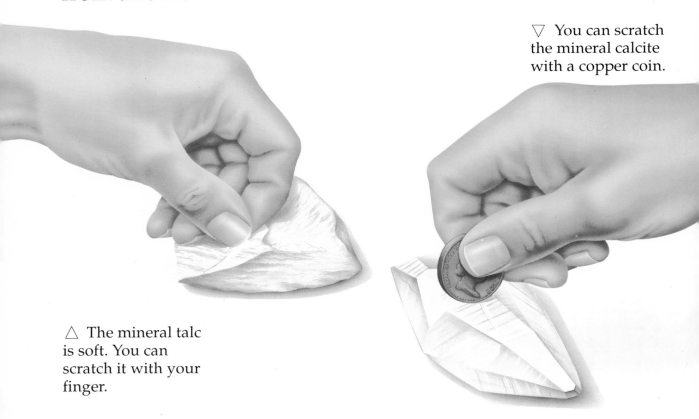

△ The mineral talc is soft. You can scratch it with your finger.

▽ The mineral quartz is hard enough to scratch glass.

▷ A special steel file is needed to scratch quartz.

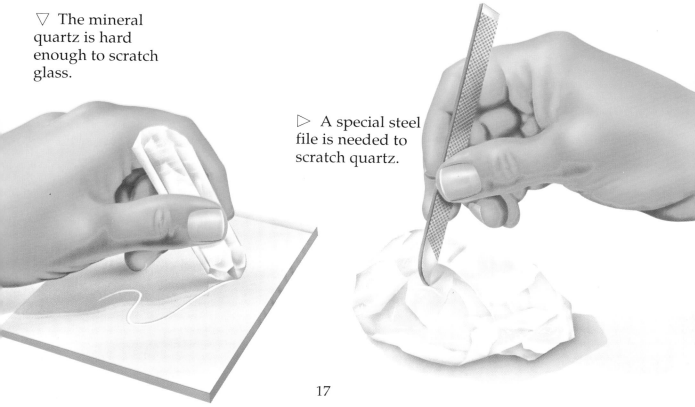

17

Crystals

If you leave a saucer of seawater in the sun, the water slowly disappears. Look through a magnifying glass, and you will see that minerals in the water have formed a crust of tiny salt **crystals**. Most minerals form crystals. Crystals of the same mineral may be very different in size.

▽ Quartz forms regular-shaped crystals with flat sides.

▽ Gypsum is a mineral used to make plaster of paris, which is used to set broken bones.

△ Sulfur occurs as crystals and as lumps in a mass of earth.

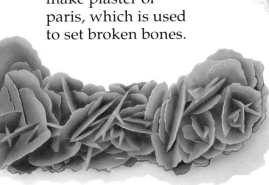

▷ Amethyst is a purple quartz. It often forms beautiful clusters of crystals.

▷ Diamond crystals usually have eight faces or sides.

▽ Zircon crystals are sometimes polished and used as jewels.

▽ Crystals of galena contain the metal lead.

Minerals and Metals

Some minerals contain useful metals. These minerals are called **ores**. We can get iron from an ore called hematite. Iron is used to make steel. Ores like these are dug out of the ground by miners. The ores are crushed or heated to make the metal. Metal can be used to make all kinds of objects, such as cars, pipes, and cans.

▽ Miners dig up metal ores from the ground.

◁ Chalcopyrite is an ore containing copper. It is used to make pipes and saucepans.

▷ Bauxite is an ore containing aluminum. It is a metal used to make cans, cars, and airplanes.

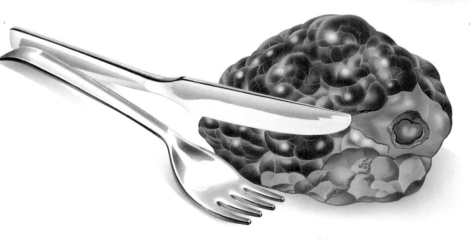

◁ Hematite is the most important ore of iron. Steel objects are made from iron.

Using Rocks and Minerals

If you crush some colored rocks and minerals, you produce powders that can be used to make paints. People once crushed the mineral hematite to produce a reddish-brown powder to make rouge.

Jewels such as rubies are used in watches with moving parts. Diamonds are used to make cutting instruments. Some jewels are used for laser surgery.

▷ Hard minerals such as rubies are used in watches that have moving parts.

▷ Cinnabar was once used to make vermilion, a bright red paint.

◁ The rock lapis lazuli was once crushed to make blue pigment or paint.

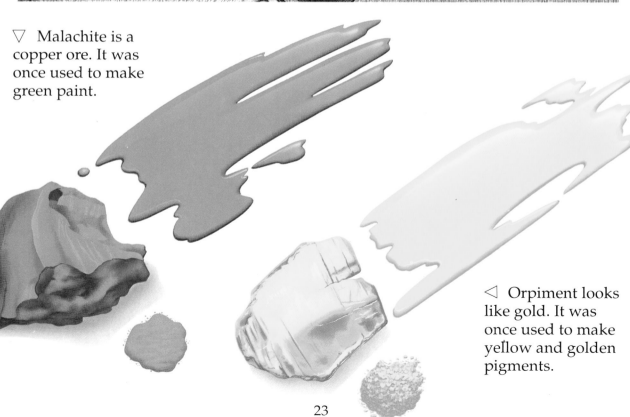

▽ Malachite is a copper ore. It was once used to make green paint.

◁ Orpiment looks like gold. It was once used to make yellow and golden pigments.

Valuable Metals

Some metals such as gold, silver, and platinum are very valuable. And they are attractive to look at. Gold, silver, and platinum are rare, since they are usually only found in small amounts. For hundreds of years gold and silver have been used for jewelry and coins. They are also used in industry and by dentists and doctors.

▷ Gold is sometimes used by dentists for capping teeth and also for fillings.

▽ Gold crystals are very rare. Gold is more often found as lumps called nuggets.

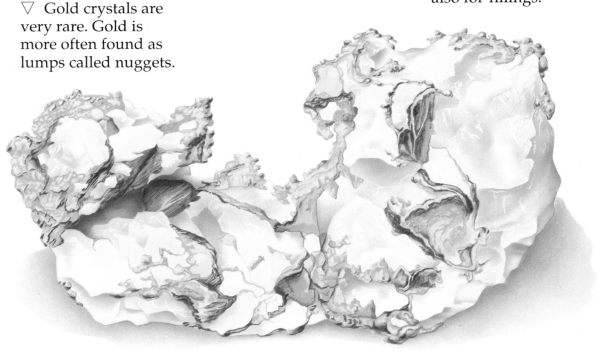

▽ Gold and silver have been used in jewelry since ancient times.

Precious Stones

Some minerals called **precious stones** are used in jewelry. Diamonds are precious stones. When they are cut and polished they have a brilliant sparkle. Some diamonds may not have any color but many are yellow. Other precious stones are rubies, which are red, and sapphires, which are blue.

▷ Precious stones are used to decorate jewelry and other valuable objects.

▷ Ruby is a rare, red form of a common mineral called corundum.

▽ Glittering stones, such as diamonds, are used in many kinds of jewelry.

▽ Emerald is a bright green form of a mineral called beryl.

△ Sapphire is another rare form of the mineral corundum.

Other Stones

There are many other beautiful minerals that can be made into jewelry. These include agate which is a striped stone, red carnelian, garnets, opal, tiger's eye, and turquoise. They are prized because of their colors which may change shade within one piece. Some minerals are large and tough enough to carve.

▷ Jewelers take great care in cutting and polishing stones.

▽ Garnets are found in metamorphic rocks. They occur in many colors.

▷ Agate is a mineral which has a striped pattern.

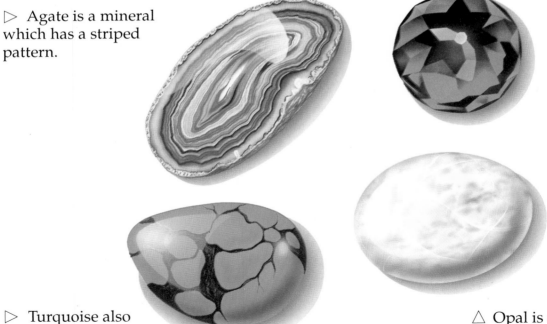

▷ Turquoise also gives its name to a blue-green color.

△ Opal is a mineral that shows rainbow colors when you turn it around.

Things to Do

- Many people collect rocks and minerals. When you visit a lake or the seashore look at the pebbles on the beach. See if you can recognize any of the rocks and minerals.

- Visit your local natural history or science museum. You can find out there what common rocks and minerals are found near your home.

- Fossil collecting is also fun. In any rocky area or near a stream look carefully at rocks. They often contain fossils. Break the rocks apart gently to reveal fossil shapes.

- City buildings are good places to see rocks and minerals. Granite covers many large buildings. Marble can be found inside buildings on the floors and walls. Many old buildings and monuments are made of limestone and sandstone.

Useful Addresses:

National Museum of Natural History
Smithsonian Institution
10th St. & Constitution Ave., N.W.
Washington, DC 20560

American Geological Institute
National Center for Earth Science Education
4220 King St.
Alexandria, VA 22302

Glossary

crust   The outer hard shell of the Earth.

crystal   A crystal is a substance that forms with regular flat surfaces. Diamonds and sulfur both form as crystals.

Earth   The planet on which we live. Earth is also the name for the soil that covers the rocks in the crust.

igneous rock   A rock formed from magma that cooled and became solid.

magma   Melted rock that is found under the Earth's surface. When it comes to the surface, it may become lava or ash.

metamorphic rock   A rock formed when another rock was heated or under great pressure.

mineral   A mineral is any substance that is not alive and that can be dug out of the ground.

ore   A mineral that contains a useful substance such as a metal.

precious stones   Stones that are rare and beautiful, such as rubies and emeralds. They are used in jewelry.

sedimentary rock   A layered rock formed from bits of sediments squeezed together.

volcano   A volcano is a hole in the surface of the Earth. It is usually shaped like a mountain. Hot melted rock and gas come out of a volcano.

Index

agate   28
amethyst   18

basalt   4-5
bauxite   21

chalcopyrite   21
chalk   10, 14-15
cinnabar   2
coal   11
conglomerate   8
crystal   18-19, 24

diamond   16, 17, 22, 26

emerald   27

feldspar   14, 15
fossil   10-11, 30

galena   19
garnet   28
gold   23, 24-25
granite   6-7, 14, 15

hematite   20, 21, 22

igneous rock   4

jewelry   24-25, 26, 28

lapis lazuli   22
limestone   10, 12, 14

malachite   23
marble   12-13
metal   20-21

metamorphic rock   12-13, 28
mica   14, 15
migmatite   12

obsidian   4
opal   28
ore   20-21
orpiment   23

polishing   6, 19, 26, 28-29
pumice   4

quartz   14, 15, 16, 17, 18

ruby   22-23, 26

sandstone   8
sapphire   27
sedimentary rock   8-9
shale   8, 12
silver   24-25
slate   12
sulfur   18

talc   16
turquoise   28

volcanic bomb   4

zircon   18

Photographic credits: Bruce Coleman (Jane Burton) 19, (Keith Gunnar) cover, 20; Eye Ubiquitous 25; FLPA (Hugh Clark) 14-15; Robert Harding Picture Library (G.M. Wilkins) 17; David Paterson 13; Science Photo Librart (David Parker) 23; Zefa cover, 5, 9, (H. Schmied) 3, (H. Grondal) 10.